To:

From:

For the Beary Best Mom

The Boyds Collection Ltd.®

Text written by Patrick Regan

**Andrews McMeel
Publishing**

Kansas City

For the Beary Best Mom

04 05 06 07 08 WKT 10 9 8 7 6 5 4 3 2

ISBN: 0-7407-4165-9

Library of Congress Control Number: 2003111243

Book design by Holly Camerlinck

For the
Beary Best Mom

♥ ♥ ♥

Dear Mom,
Sometimes I get so caught up in the
hustle and bustle of life that I forget to
remember what's most important.

That's when I sit down
and think about the things and people
I care about most.

Know what?
You're always the first one
that pops into my head.

Which is really no surprise,
because you've always been first.
Yours was the first face I saw
the day I was born.

When I took my first wobbly steps
(and had my first fall),
you were there to catch me.

You were the first one to read me
bedtime stories and snuggle me to sleep.

And, of course, you dressed me
in my first silly Halloween costume.

You were my very first love—and that's
something that will never change.

♥ ♥ ♥

I can't think of a time when you
weren't there for me.

♥ ♥ ♥

Through countless recitals . . .

And lots of school programs . . .

You were always there
cheering me on.

And even if I wasn't quite
an all-star, you always made me
feel like one.

You were always watching out for me.
In the wintertime, you bundled me up
snug and warm.

And in the summer, you never
let me outside without sunscreen
and a proper sun hat.
(Whether I wanted it or not!)

FEEL BETTER!

Through tummy aches and boo-boos . . .

Hurt feelings . . .

And all those unfortunate little incidents
and accidents of childhood . . .

Your love was always the best medicine.

I know that over the years I've been
the cause of some sleepless nights . . .

But when I made mistakes,
you graciously accepted my apologies.

You gently corrected me when I acted like a little devil . . .

♥   ♥   ♥

And treated me to ice cream when
I was good (and even sometimes
when I wasn't so good!).

♥   ♥   ♥

I realize now, Mom, how you
always put your family's needs
ahead of your own.

I still can't understand
how you did it all.

You were always finding new ways to
add beauty and joy to our lives.

You encouraged our creativity and
filled every day with fun.

And all the while,
you kept the house in order . . .

Your children presentable . . .

And somehow managed to make a
nutritious, home-cooked dinner every night
(a dinner you were always the
last to eat, of course).

So thanks, Mom, for teaching me
more than any teacher ever has.
Important lessons like:

When life's got you down,
change your perspective.

♥ ♥ ♥

Give your heart freely
to those you love.

♥ ♥ ♥

Always put your best foot forward.

Celebrate the joys of every season.

And, most of all, take good care
of the ones you love.

Thanks for everything, Mama Bear.
I love you.